I Can See
At the Park

By Czeena Devera

2 I see a playground at the park.

I see a sandbox at the park.

4

I see a bench at the park.

I see a grill at the park.

I see grass at the park.

I see a bike at the park.

7

I see a kite at the park.

I see a squirrel at the park.

I see a picnic at the park.

I see a pond at the park.

I see a seesaw at the park.

I see friends at the park.

Word List

park	grass	pond
playground	bike	seesaw
sandbox	kite	friends
bench	squirrel	
grill	picnic	

82 Words

I see a playground at the park.
I see a sandbox at the park.
I see a bench at the park.
I see a grill at the park.
I see grass at the park.
I see a bike at the park.
I see a kite at the park.
I see a squirrel at the park.
I see a picnic at the park.
I see a pond at the park.
I see a seesaw at the park.
I see friends at the park.

Published in the United States of America by Cherry Lake Publishing
Ann Arbor, Michigan
www.cherrylakepublishing.com

Photo Credits: © Sergiy Kuzmin/Shutterstock.com, front cover, 1, 12; © Eric Isselee/Shutterstock.com, back cover, 15; © MongPro/Shutterstock.com, 2; © Gorlov-KV/Shutterstock.com, 3; © Marso/Shutterstock.com, 4; © Arne Beruldsen/Shutterstock.com, 5; © Songdech Kothmongkol/Shutterstock.com, 6; © Naratip Bamrungrat/Dreamstime.com, 7; © DrPilulkin/Shutterstock.com, 8; © Simpelvel/Shutterstock.com, 9; © Alain Lacroix/Dreamstime.com, 10; © TreasureGalore/Shutterstock.com, 11; © Monkey Business Images/Shutterstock.com, 13

Copyright © 2019 by Cherry Lake Publishing

All rights reserved. No part of this book may be reproduced or utilized
in any form or by any means without written permission from the publisher.

Cherry Blossom Press is an imprint of Cherry Lake Publishing.

Library of Congress Cataloging-in-Publication Data has been filed and is available at catalog.loc.gov

Printed in the United States of America
Corporate Graphics

CHERRY BLOSSOM PRESS